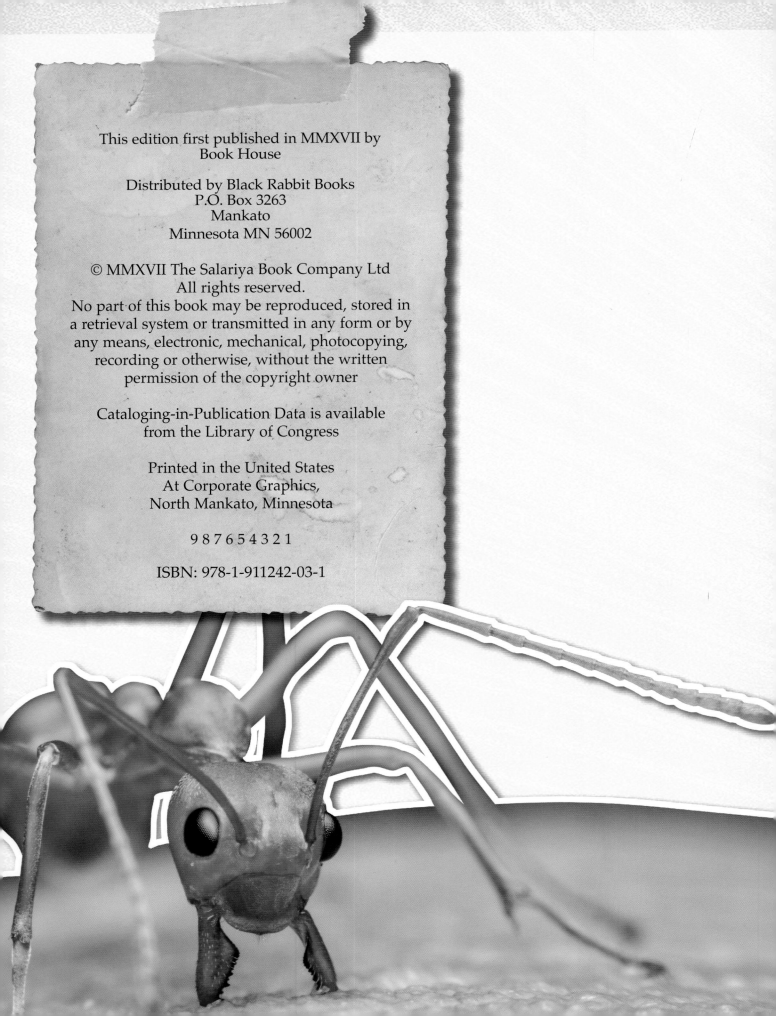

This edition first published in MMXVII by
Book House

Distributed by Black Rabbit Books
P.O. Box 3263
Mankato
Minnesota MN 56002

Cataloging-in-Publication Data is available
from the Library of Congress

Printed in the United States
At Corporate Graphics,
North Mankato, Minnesota

9 8 7 6 5 4 3 2 1

ISBN: 978-1-911242-03-1

ANT

David Miller

UP CLOSE & SCARY

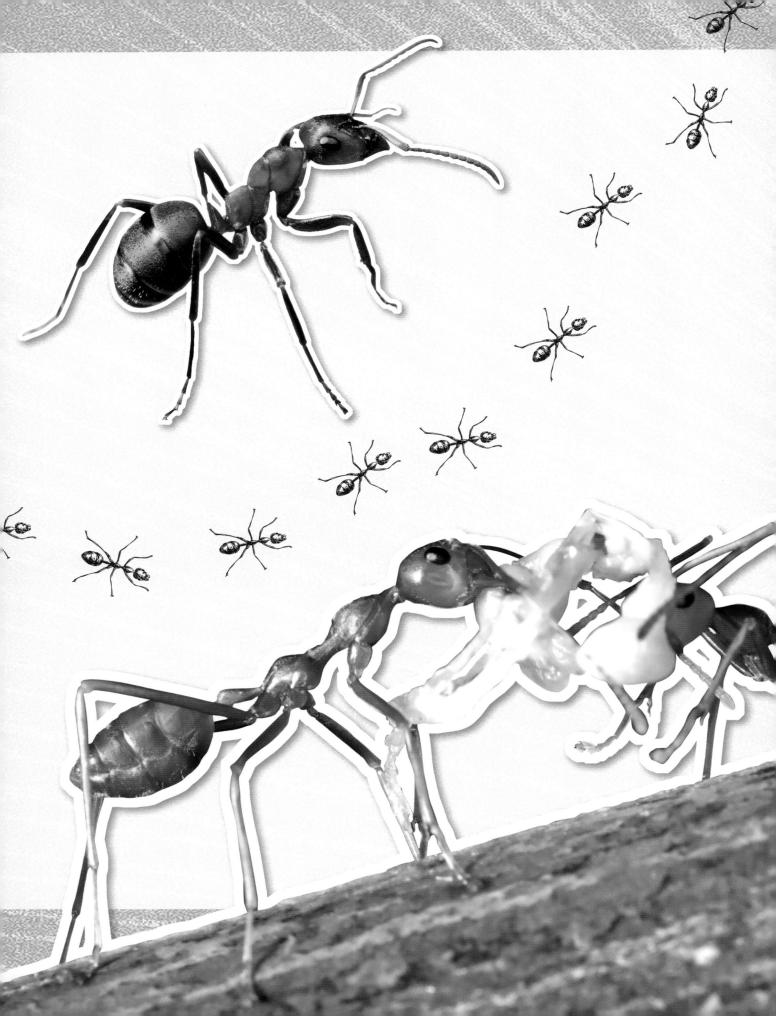

Contents

Ants

Ants live in almost every corner of our planet. They can be black, brown, yellow, green, or blue. The scariest thing about ants is that millions of them can live in one colony. They will attack anything in their path. Most ants are workers. They build nests, collect food, and do many different jobs. Soldier ants form the army. They will attack if the colony or nest is threatened. Queens are the most important ants in the colony. Their job is to lay eggs that will hatch into a new generation.

This worker ant tends to the other ants, including the queen.

Soldier ant

Queen ant

Ants in a colony look different because they have different jobs to do.

The Body

An ant's body has three main parts: the head, thorax, and abdomen. The eyes, mouth, and antennae are on the head. The legs are attached to the thorax and the abdomen is where food is digested.

Superpowers

Once a year some of the young ants develop wings. The young queen ants mate with the fastest fliers. Afterward, each queen starts a new colony. The queens no longer need wings so they bite them off!

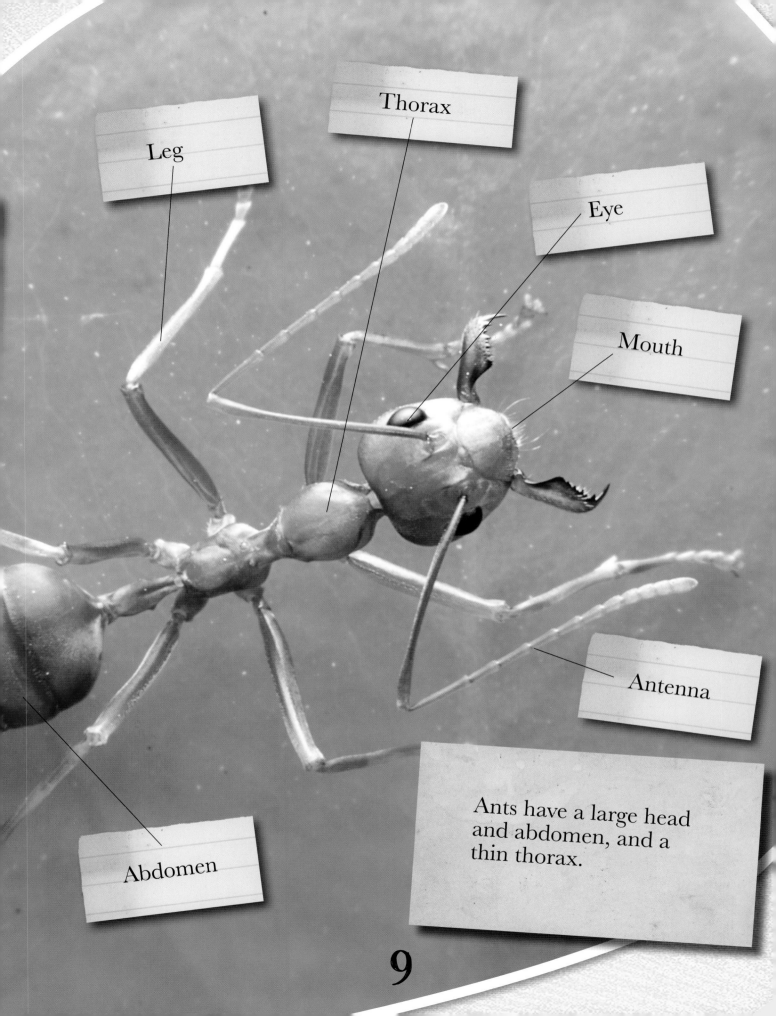

Leg

Thorax

Eye

Mouth

Antenna

Abdomen

Ants have a large head and abdomen, and a thin thorax.

9

The Abdomen

An ant's round abdomen is covered in short bristles. The abdomen contains two stomachs. One, called the crop, is for storing food for the colony. The other stomach is smaller. It is for storing an ant's own food.

Superpowers

Honeypot ants live in deserts and can super-size! The large worker ants, called repletes, eat so much that their abdomens swell up as big as cherries. These overstuffed abdomens become a food store for the dry season.

Abdomen

Glands in the abdomen release a smell that other ants recognize. Ants leave a scent trail.

When ants look like they are kissing, they are feeding each other! One is passing food from its abdomen into the other's mouth.

Waist

Ants tap their abdomen on the nest to warn the colony of danger.

The Head

An ant's brain is quite big for an insect. It takes in all the information from its antennae, eyes, and other sense organs. Ants have two large compound eyes. They also have tiny simple eyes on their head.

Superpowers

An ant is smart for its size because it has a big brain. If a human brain was on the same scale, it would weigh about 20 pounds (9 kilograms)!

12

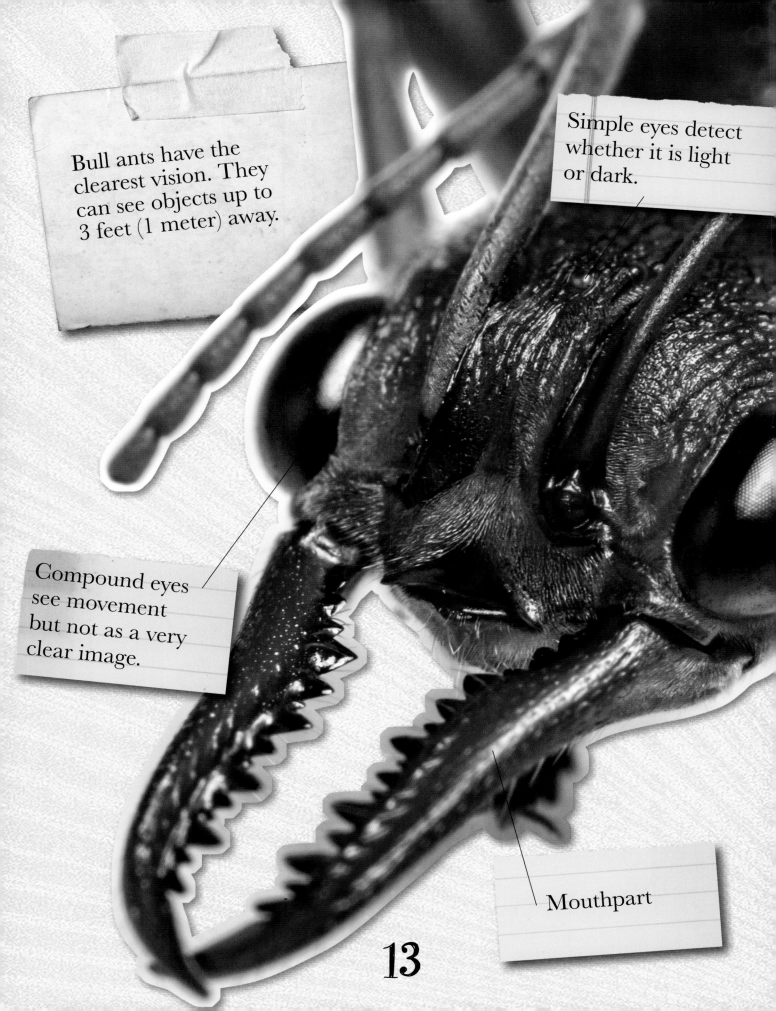

Bull ants have the clearest vision. They can see objects up to 3 feet (1 meter) away.

Simple eyes detect whether it is light or dark.

Compound eyes see movement but not as a very clear image.

Mouthpart

13

The Antennae

An ant's antennae are covered with tiny sense organs. Antennae help it to smell and touch things. A sense of smell is important for recognizing other ants. If an ant smells like the colony, the other ants welcome it. If not, they may fight.

Superpowers

Fire ants dig underground nests where they race through narrow, crowded tunnels. Their antennae help them to avoid bumping into ants coming the other way. If humans had antennae, they would never bump into people in crowded streets!

14

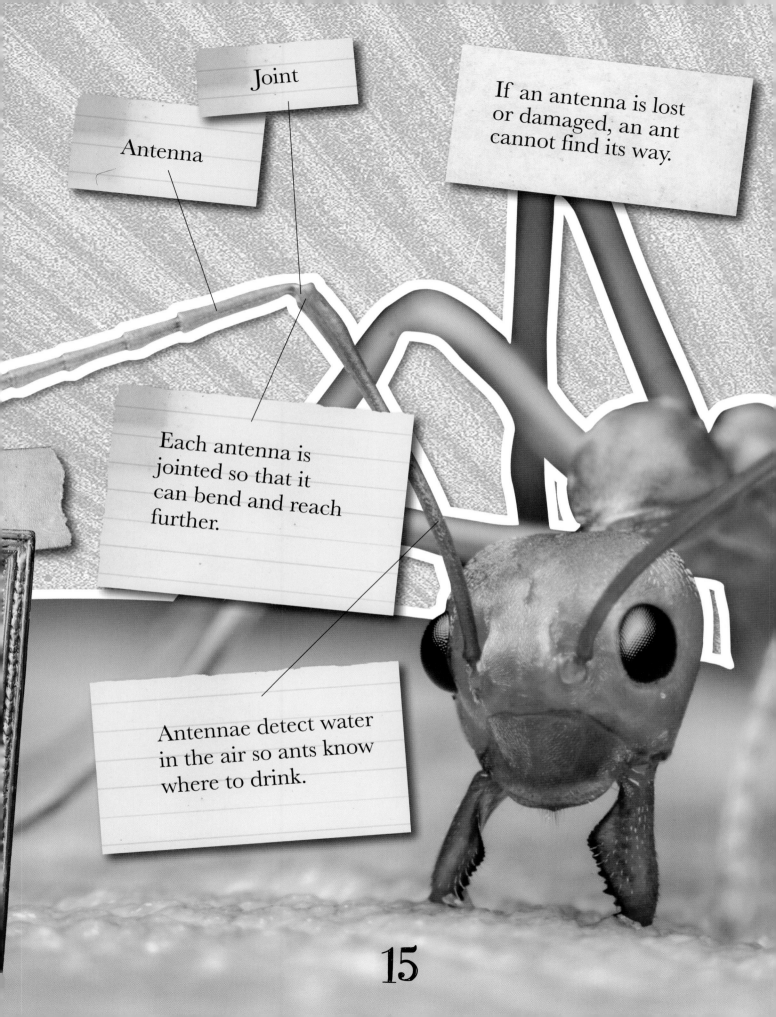

Antenna

Joint

If an antenna is lost or damaged, an ant cannot find its way.

Each antenna is jointed so that it can bend and reach further.

Antennae detect water in the air so ants know where to drink.

15

The Mouth

Ants have strong jaws called mandibles. They grip like pliers, pierce like daggers, and dig like spades. Ants use them to attack and eat prey or to carry things back to the colony. They also use them to build nests.

Antenna

Mandible

An ant uses its mandibles like hands, to grips things.

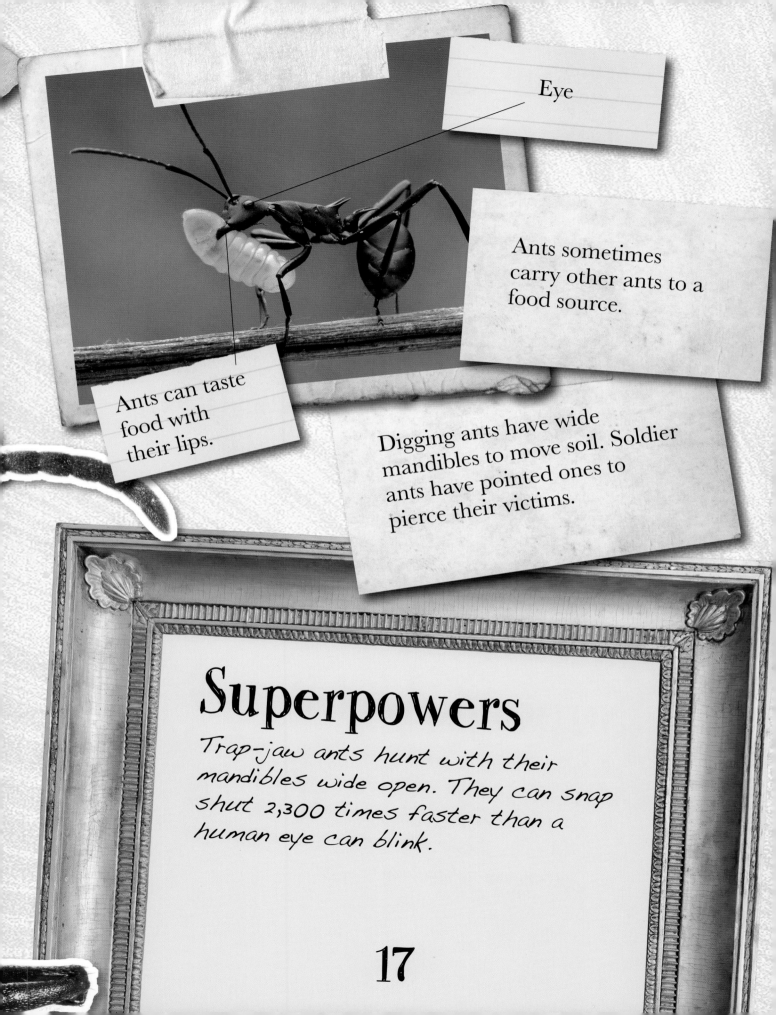

Eye

Ants can taste food with their lips.

Ants sometimes carry other ants to a food source.

Digging ants have wide mandibles to move soil. Soldier ants have pointed ones to pierce their victims.

Superpowers

Trap-jaw ants hunt with their mandibles wide open. They can snap shut 2,300 times faster than a human eye can blink.

17

The Legs

Ants are fast movers. They have six jointed legs with tiny claws that help them grip. As one leg lifts, another touches the ground, so three legs are always on the floor. An ant uses the hairs on its front legs for cleaning.

Superpowers

Sahara desert ants live in one of the hottest places on Earth. When they leave their nest, they easily find their way back. They remember exactly how many steps they have taken!

18

Leg

Joint

An ant's claws help it to climb without slipping.

An ant's legs each have five sections connected by joints.

19

The Stinger

An ant's stinger is the pointed bit at the end of its abdomen. The stinger injects venom under the skin of prey or a threatening animal. Some ants have stingers that shoot venom into a predator's eyes.

Superpowers

Jumper ants and bulldog ants can kill people. These aggressive insects bite, and then deliver a painful, venomous sting. People who are allergic to the venom can die within 15 minutes.

20

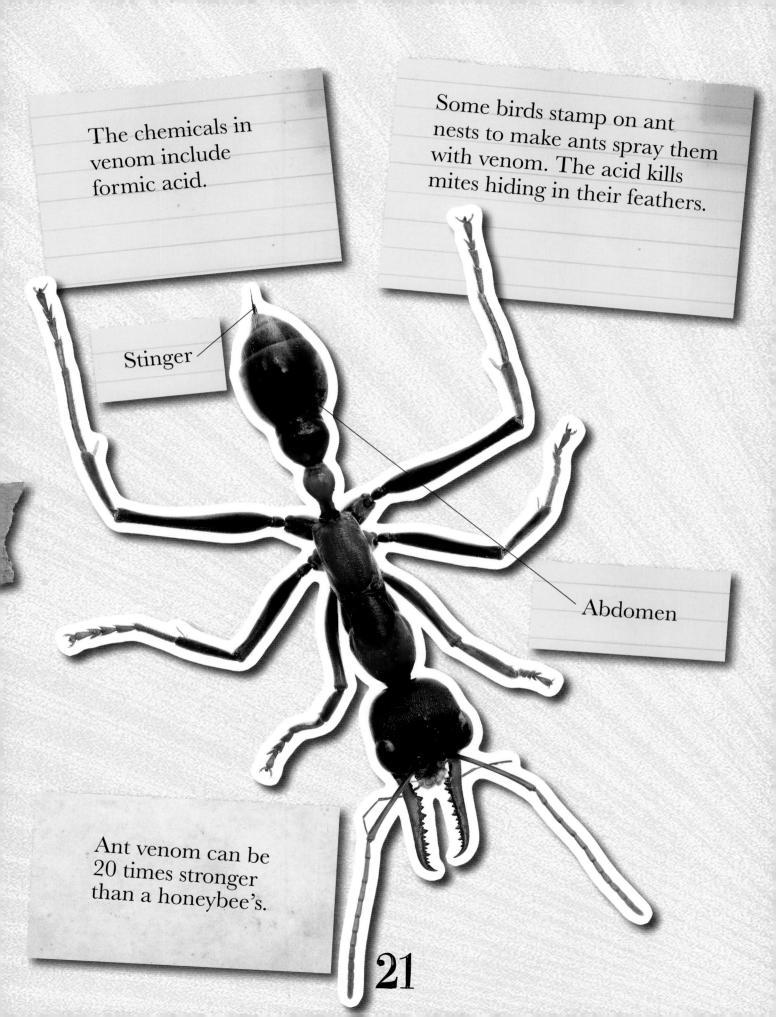

The chemicals in venom include formic acid.

Some birds stamp on ant nests to make ants spray them with venom. The acid kills mites hiding in their feathers.

Stinger

Abdomen

Ant venom can be 20 times stronger than a honeybee's.

Weaver Ants

Ants make many different types of nest. Weaver ants make leaf nests. Many worker ants unite to pull the leaves together. Then, holding the ant larvae carefully, they tap them with their antennae. This makes the larvae produce silk to stick the leaves together.

Weaver ants make a large colony of nests in one tree.

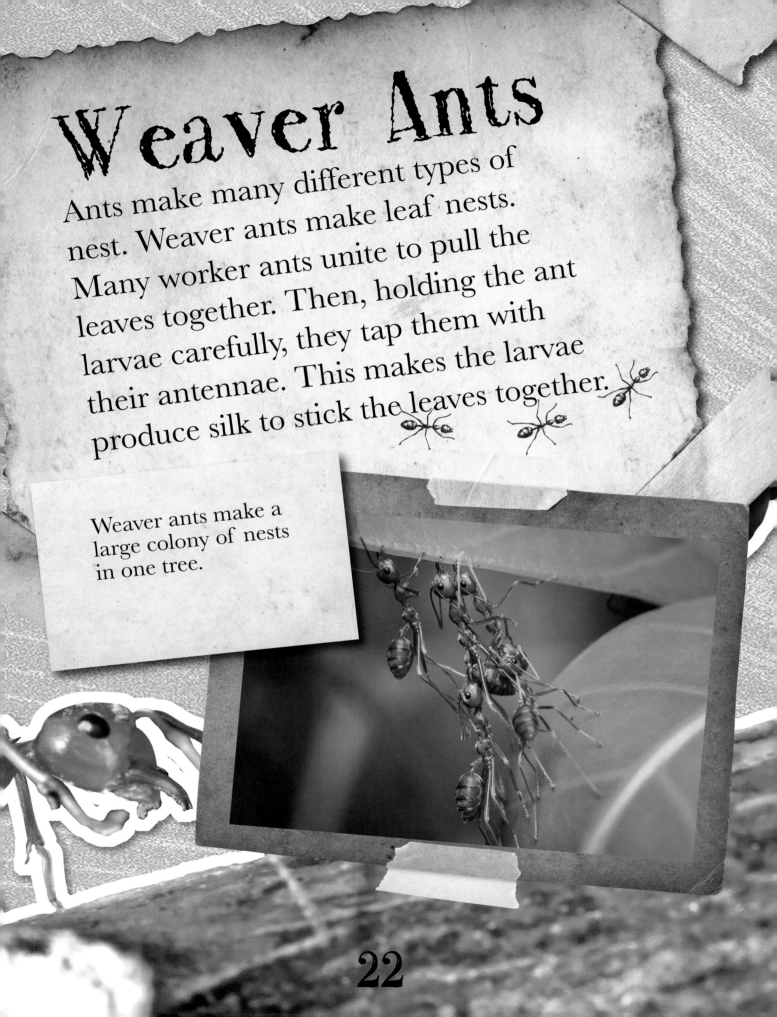

Worker

Silk

Weaver ants' leaf nests are usually football-sized.

Mandibles

Superpowers

Weaver ants have long, strong legs. They can lift up to 100 times their own weight. If you were this strong, you could lift a minibus full of people!

23

Thorn Ants

The big thorns of a tropical acacia tree have a nasty surprise inside—thorn ants! Ants hollow-out the base of the thorn and live in it. They like to eat the acacia tree's sweet nectar. They sting any animal or bug that tries to feed on its leaves.

Thorn

Ant

Leaf

Acacia trees can whistle. When ants move out, the empty thorns whistle as the wind blows through them.

Superpowers

Thorn ants are smart! They nip off the buds on branch tips to stop them growing toward nearby trees. Other ants cannot climb across.

25

Driver Ants

A column of driver ants is a scary sight. Traveling through an African forest, a vast column of 20 million driver ants can be up to 3 feet (1 meter) wide. They eat any worms and insects in their path, and sometimes even bigger animals like snakes and horses.

Superpowers

When a driver ant's mandibles slice through a victim's flesh, they lock together. People in African forests sometimes hold the edges of a cut together, then let the ant's mandibles "staple" their wound.

Soldiers on the outside of the column defend the worker ants in the middle.

The worker ants carry food, eggs, and larvae.

A column of driver ants can be 328 feet (100 meters) long.

A column of tiny driver ants travels about 46 feet (14 meters) per hour.

27

That's Scary!

For each human there are thousands of ants. The reason they are so widespread is because ants are clever and efficient, and they work well together in large groups. Ants do sting, and can cause damage, but they are very useful insects. They kill pests on food crops, and help to clear up by eating dead animals and food waste. By digging the soil they make it more fertile, so plants grow better. Some ants pollinate flowers, too. The scariest thing about ants is how much our planet needs them to remain healthy.

Some ants are smart survival experts. They escape floods by forming rafts and bridges!

Leaf-cutter ants bite off bits of leaves. They turn it into compost to grow mushrooms to feed the colony.

Glossary

Abdomen stomach.

Allergic unusual reaction in someone's body, such as a rash.

Antennae feelers on an insect's head, used to feel and taste.

Chemical a substance made by a chemical process.

Colony a group of animals of the same type that live together in one place.

Compound eyes eyes made up of many lenses.

Crop stomach used to store food.

Fertile capable of growing many, healthy crops.

Formic acid type of smelly, burning chemical.

Glands body part that produces special chemicals, such as venom.

Jointed where two separately moving bones or body parts meet.

Larvae the wingless stage of insects when first hatched.

Mate the way animals create new versions of themselves.

Mites small animals related to spiders.

Nectar a sugary juice found in flowers.

Pollinate when pollen moves from one flower to another flower of the same kind to make new plants.

Predator an animal that catches other animals to eat.

Prey an animal eaten by others.

Queen ant the female head of an ant colony, and the only one who can lay eggs.

Sense organs body parts responsible for the five senses: hearing, sight, smell, taste, and touch.

Silk sticky material produced by ant larvae to wrap themselves into cocoons.

Simple eyes eyes with only one lens.

Soldier ants aggressive ants with big jaws that defend the colony.

Stinger body part that injects or sprays venom.

Thorax body part between the head and abdomen.

Venom poisonous fluid used to kill prey or warn off predators.

Workers ants that collect food, tend to the queen and others, and build nests. Most ants in a colony are workers.

Index